Clean and Prosperous

How Cleanliness Means More Productivity
and Increased ROI for your Business

By Scott Romero

Clean and Prosperous

How Cleanliness Means More Productivity and Increased ROI for your Business

www.cleanandprosperous.com

By Scott Romero

City Wide of Memphis
gocitywide.com/memphis

Clean and Prosperous

.

Table of Contents

Introduction

I know what you're thinking – a book about cleaning? Sounds like a boring topic, doesn't it? Isn't cleaning just a matter of mopping the floors, wiping down some tables, and doing a little dusting? What could possibly be said that requires a whole book about the topic?

Actually, cleaning is an important and interesting subject. Think about it. Would you shop in a store that is filthy? Would you eat in a restaurant infested with cockroaches and with floors covered in garbage? Would you want to work in an environment so dirty that it's hazardous to your health?

Clients and the public use cleanliness as one way to evaluate how well a business is succeeding. When I shop in a grocery store, I expect that the floors are swept, the shelves are clean, and the produce isn't covered with insects or filth. A dirty grocery store means the food isn't healthy or desirable, a restaurant with insects crawling around is never a good sign, and a business with clutter translates to one that is not well managed.

A lack of cleanliness causes other problems and directly affects your P&L bottom line. A cluttered workplace with garbage on the floor can cause slip and fall accidents, dusty air ducts can result in a greater occurrence of illnesses and allergies among employees, and general disarray can lose business.

Let's look at some of the ways that a lack of cleanliness affects business.

- **Employees get sick more often**. Dirt and filth breed disease and attract pests such as insects and rodents.
- **Filthy facilities turn away customers**. Think about the last time you were in a restaurant or a gas station and you found the restroom was just plain nasty. Did you want to go back to that establishment?
- **Attracting new employees is more difficult**. It's quite natural for people to want to work in a clean environment, and if they see that your office is dirty during the hiring process, they are more likely to accept a different offer and work somewhere else.

- **Allergies can result in lawsuits and lost productivity**. Employees with allergic reactions to dust can demand ADA concessions and even file lawsuits if their concerns are not addressed.
- **Inspections can become more difficult to pass**. Stacks of papers and books, garbage on the floor, old building materials and uneaten food can be an indicator to inspectors that there are deeper problems. Fire inspectors, for example, can interpret uncleanliness as a sign that they need to look closer at the wiring and the location of flammable materials.

What do you know about cleaning people? When you picture a janitor, do you think of someone who is down on their luck with no other options in life except to clean the floors and scrub the toilets?

Look at many movies or books, and you'll see or read about stereotypical janitors with unkempt hair, unwashed clothes, who smell bad and have slovenly habits.

Nothing could be further from the truth. These businesspeople are among the most underappreciated workers in any industry. Even so, as a rule, they are treated with disrespect and avoided when possible.

But think about it. The cleaning person has one of the hardest jobs possible. They typically work 2 to 3 jobs, often holding down a full-time position in the day, going home to eat, and then continuing to clean buildings all night long. They often do this without any thanks or even acknowledgment of their vital contribution to any business.

Cleaning people have families just like everyone else. In fact, this might surprise you, but janitors are among the most highly entrepreneurial type of people that exist. Many of them own their own cleaning company and run their own business. They do everything themselves, operating as a one-person shop.

These entrepreneurs feel a strong sense of pride and are highly motivated to provide the best possible cleaning services because they understand the importance of what they do. They know that a well cleaned office makes a business look good, is more likely to attract customers and employees, and is overall a healthier place to work.

I wrote this book to help business owners make their businesses more profitable and provide better and safer places to work in by using effective cleaning processes. As you read, you'll find out how you can save money in the long run related to cleaning and other building maintenance, and you'll learn what policies and procedures you should put in place.

My Story

If you've ever been to Big Bear Lake in California, then you know how beautiful an environment can be. The San Bernardino Mountains provided a wonderful place for me to grow up in the beauty of nature in a small-town environment.

I learned people can live in harmony with nature and each other. The advantage of a small town is that everybody knows everybody, and everyone is willing to help.

I think I was lucky growing up that way in that place. It was a magical time for me, and because of the environment I innately understood that people need to work together and can still enjoy the advantages of living in a natural, safe environment.

A big lesson that I learned from my father is that a person's respect is earned by a strong sense of integrity and honesty. I've carried those teachings through my entire life, and every day I strive to be the best that I can be for my family, community, and business.

***

I know it sounds corny, but I began my entrepreneurial journey with a lemonade stand in my front yard. Day after day, week after week in the heat of the summer, I sat in a chair under an umbrella, with a bucket full of ice at my side and a pile of lemons in a basket on the table in front of me.

The neighbors made special trips to stop by my stand on hot afternoons, so they could get a drink of cool, delicious lemonade with ice. I charged a dime per cup and put the money into a savings account which I intended to use to start my own business when I grew up.

Other businesses followed, mowing lawns, cleaning garages, and anything else that I could do to help the neighbors and earn money for my future.

My parents kept their home clean and well organized. I learned from them that "cleanliness is next to godliness" and that you can tell a lot about a person by how clean their surroundings are. A disorganized home means a disorganized life; a filthy home has even similar connotations.

***

In my late teens, I became a sales manager at Leroy's Ski Shop, and quickly worked my way up to a team leader position. My role was customer service, and I took that seriously. I knew, even at that young age, that customers are the lifeblood of business.

I spent four years improving their standards for customer service and helping the store with its marketing campaigns and even revamped the inventory floor merchandising plan. While I was there, I'm proud to say that sales increased between 15% and 25% per month. My team and I worked together to improve the business and to ensure that our customers enjoyed coming to our shop.

Moving on to a position as Sales Manager and Regional Sales Director for Big Bear Choppers, I became responsible for 25 stores that carried our products. That was a lot of responsibility, but since the team was phenomenal, I was up to the task.

In 2009, I joined the military and became a Fire Protection Specialist. I wanted to serve my country, to aid in protecting our great nation from those who intended to do it harm, and I felt this was the best way to do that.

Operating out of Shindad Air Base in Afghanistan while in the military, I developed and inspected fire protection systems for the entire base. This required over 250 pre-final and final construction inspections to ensure FFP compliance. This was needed for optimum safety of the base personnel under combat conditions.

Later, as a civilian contractor at Columbus Air Force Base, I continued serving my country by performing inspections, training team members, and even aiding in unexploded bomb ordinance situations.

During this time working for the military, I educated over 4,000 civilians in the importance of fire safety and was the supervisor for 56 personnel during search and rescue mass casualty situations.

All this experience reinforced that integrity and honesty are vital parts of survival and business. It's impossible for a team to work effectively without those characteristics.

I learned that I am a passionate entrepreneur with a fascination of the thrill of business. My true love is business-to-business sales and providing top-notch service, which results in obtaining lifelong, satisfied customers.

In June 2017, I decided it was time to put my talents to work and fulfill my passion for leading an effective team. After much research, I found that I could contribute to the effectiveness and bottom line of businesses by helping them keep their environment clean and organized.

With that understanding, I started the Memphis branch of City Wide Maintenance, helping building owners and property managers with over 20 services from maintaining their parking lots to cleaning their offices to caring for their lawns. My goal is to save those clients their most valuable asset – which is time – at a reasonable cost.

Business owners want to connect with their sales representatives and create a personal relationship with them. Additionally, discerning customers prefer one source for all their needs. By providing this and streamlining the process we reduce their stress and help them achieve their goals.

The best way to sell is to be a great leader with a fantastic team. My philosophy is leaders must lead from the front lines and prove to team members that the business is aligned with their personal interests. It's vital to empower the team to have integrity and do what's best for the customer.

The Importance of Cleaning

Let's say you are job hunting, and you've narrowed it down to two offers. One company was impressively clean – the floors were sparkling, and everything was in its place. The other was a literal pigsty, with open pizza boxes on the floors and uneaten food on desks. All other things being equal, which job offer would you accept?

I'm sure that everyone has had the displeasure of having to use nasty bathrooms at gas stations or markets. Did that make you want to continue doing business with those companies? Did you feel good about giving them your money? After all, doesn't it seem kind of basic to keep the bathrooms at least moderately clean most of the time?

The cleanliness of your business speaks volumes about the health of your business. You may not notice if the place is clean, but you'll certainly be aware if it's filthy.

I was talking to Nick, a fellow business owner, and he said, "we'd been negotiating for over a week. It was some hard negotiations, but I was finally happy with the contract. I drove down to their office to sign the papers for delivery of almost 500 computer systems. Stepping inside the building, after a long, hard commute, I wasn't impressed. I didn't expect marble floors or anything, but I don't think it's out of line for a business to clean the restrooms now and then, and at least pick up the garbage from the lobby. I decided I didn't want to do business with them and didn't sign the contract. Why not? Because if they can't even keep their office clean, how can I expect them to a good job on the computers they were delivering?"

I think you'd be amazed at how often this kind of thing happens.

Walk around and look over your own business, whether you're an employee or the owner. What message does it deliver?

An unclean office harms a business.

- Customers feel uneasy in unclean surroundings, which makes them less likely to do business.

- Dust and filth can cause allergies, especially over time.
- Pests such as insects and rodents can become a problem.
- Employee morale goes down.
- Hiring new employees can become more difficult.
- The frequency of employee illnesses can increase.

A friend of mine worked in a small business in North Long Beach, California, located in a small office off a main thoroughfare. Before the business was open, the office was completely renovated with new paneling, carpets, lighting and furniture. When the doors opened for the first time, the place was immaculately clean and projected an image of confidence and expertise.

A few years later, the carpet appeared worn from use and was dirty from lack of cleaning. There were scuff marks on the floors, and the desks and shelves were stuffed with broken equipment, wires, stacks of paper and dusty books. It didn't look terrible – just messy and unkempt.

However, the image of the business changed because of the office environment. No longer did you get a feeling of confidence and ability when you walked through the door; instead, it projected a feeling of tiredness and a vague incompetence.

At the same time, employee turnover increased, and it became more difficult to acquire new customers. Money always seemed to be tight and of course cleaning was not considered a priority.

Eventually, the owner hired a cleaning crew to come out and scrub down the office. Overnight, the feeling of confidence and expertise returned; employees again felt motivated to come to work each day. Customers were happy to visit, and vendors didn't seem to be in as much of a hurry to leave.

Cleaning makes a huge difference to a business.

INCREASED SECURITY

I was surprised to learn from a friend of mine who is a computer security expert that a cluttered and unkempt office is more insecure than a clean one.

"Let me give you an example," my security friend told me. "I performed an audit of a company, you know, checked out their security, and one thing I found was a number of files strewn over the top of a messy desk. I inspected those files and found several confidential financial reports. These were not locked away in a file cabinet where they would be safe."

"In another instance," he continued, "I found several cases where people working in the HR department had piled files on top of their desks, out of the open, containing sensitive and confidential employee information."

"In either case, if these papers had been found by an auditor, the company could have been in hot water. Worse yet, if they had been discovered by a competitor an even worse situation could have resulted."

One thing I found in all my years of office cleaning is people commonly write passwords and usernames on sticky notes, which they then tape to the side of their computer screens. This is an obvious security problem, because it grants access to anyone who happens to sit at their desk. Cleaners could be instructed to remove and destroy any sticky notes they find attached to computer screens, under keyboards, or hidden inside desk drawers.

INCREASE PRODUCTIVITY

A clean environment increases productivity. In a cluttered office, people must spend time searching for files, finding equipment and shuffling things around. I know that doesn't seem like much, but it adds up over time.

"Every time I had to reach client files," Susan told me, "I had to move boxes out of the way. It was such a waste of time, and the boxes were heavy. But it just seemed easier to put up with the hassle a little bit each day than to take the time to move the boxes into a closet or something."

Jim, an employee at the same company, mentioned, "I just pile all of the folders for each client on top of my desk. Whenever I need something, I shuffle through the folders until I find it."

An interesting exercise is to ask each of your employees to record where they spend their time during a typical workday. Just have them write down everything they do, no matter how small, throughout the day. Once you have the results, look through their lists, and you'll get a pretty good idea of where their time is going. Multiply the minutes of lost time every hour times the number of employees to find out how much time is being wasted each day. That amount is probably a lot larger than you think.

BETTER HYGIENE

Cluttered and unclean spaces attract pests such as rodents and insects. Spoiled food in the kitchen and dirty restrooms are hotbeds for germs and diseases.

Did you know phones, whether they are cell phones or desk phones, contain more germs and potential for disease than your average toilet seat? (Adams, 2017)

The cleanliness of the work environment directly affects the health of your employees.

There is more to a clean workspace than just cleaning up clutter, vacuuming, and scrubbing down the restrooms and kitchen. To maintain good hygiene, cleaning techniques must be used to create a relatively germ-free environment for your employees.

For example, wiping down countertops in the kitchen makes them look good, but it doesn't do anything to kill germs and prevent disease. To do that, professional cleaners use disinfectants and antibacterial agents to scrub down areas with a high potential to cause infection.

These techniques will result in a workplace that is less likely to infect your employees, visitors and others with diseases. The incidence of colds, flu's and other illnesses will decrease, and overall your workforce will become healthier and happier. This will lead to higher productivity.

Reduced Stress

Most people don't understand that clutter increases stress levels. When you enter a room that is disorganized or filthy, don't you instantly feel uneasy and under stress?

Stress lowers productivity because it makes people feel anxious, as if there is some undefined danger coming from somewhere.

By keeping your office clean, you're helping your employees to feel like they are in a safe environment, which effectively reduces their anxiety and stress. This allows them to focus more on doing their job instead of worrying about some undefined threat.

Save Money

A commercial cleaning company not only improves the look of your business and the impression that your customers receive, but it also saves you money.

When an office is cleaned regularly and thoroughly, small problems are addressed before they become large ones, and thus are much less expensive to handle.

For example, if carpets are cleaned regularly, small stains are removed as a matter of course. This prevents them from being ground into the carpet, essentially being embedded in the fibers, which makes the stains difficult if not impossible to remove. The result is cleaned carpets will need to be replaced less often.

Cleaning also reduces incidents from rodents and insects, which can damage your building, paper, and even electronics and wiring. By cleaning regularly, bits of food, spilled drinks, and standing water don't have a chance to breed bacteria and attract pests.

Basically, regular cleaning prevents small, generally minor issues from becoming major problems. Furniture will last longer, carpets won't need to be replaced as often, cabinetry won't have water damage, and other types of damage will be reduced or eliminated entirely.

INCREASE CREATIVITY

A study published in the Journal of Consumer Research (Zhu, 2013), suggested that clutter undermines people's ability to persevere through difficult tasks. 103 student participants were asked to sit in a room that was either clean or cluttered and asked to solve an unsolvable geometry puzzle. Each person was timed by the researchers to find out how persistent they were in the face of frustration.

Those in a neat environment spent 1,117 seconds on the task on average, while people who were in the cluttered environment spent 669 seconds. The researchers believe that working in a clean space helps people feel unburdened by the clutter and more mentally capable to persevere through a difficult problem.

CUSTOMERS FEEL MORE CONFIDENT

The cleanliness of your office sends a message to your customers. If they see you have a clean office, the message is:

- Your business is confident.
- You will do a good job or deliver a good product.
- Your people care about the job they do.
- You make sure that the "little things" get handled.

- Your business has a healthy company culture.

On the other hand, and unkempt or filthy office sends a different message.

- Your business is having money problems.
- Your employees don't care about customers.
- Your company culture is not healthy.
- The "little things" will slip through the cracks.
- You may not do a good job, or your products may be faulty.

Which message would you rather deliver to your customers?

THE INCIDENCE OF DUST AND FILTH RELATED ALLERGIES IS REDUCED

Many people have allergic reactions to substances such as dust, chemicals, cloth, leather and other things. There are many symptoms of these kind of reactions. Some of them mimic the flu or cold, and others result in difficulty breathing, hives, tiredness, diarrhea, headaches, and a whole plethora of other symptoms.

Contaminants cause allergic reactions, and this makes employees feel ill and lowers their productivity. Employees who have allergies to substances in office environments tend to take more sick days as well.

Where do these allergies come from?

- dust
- wood particles
- paints
- solvents
- cleaning fluids
- and just about anything else

One of the most common causes of allergies is dust, and this is a problem because dust accumulates everywhere and there isn't much you can do to completely eliminate it. You can, however, reduce the amount of it in the environment.

Professional cleaning companies understand where dust accumulates and use special equipment to help prevent or reduce the amount of dust that is thrown into the air.

"I couldn't figure out why I was always sick," Jane, an employee at a legal office told me. "I tried going to doctors until they looked at me like I was crazy. One day I'm doing fine, and the next my skin had broken out in ugly hives and rashes. It was very disconcerting, and I was convinced I had some kind of serious illness. One night I worked late and got into a conversation with one of the cleaning crew. After noticing that my skin was covered with those ugly red blotches, she asked a few questions. She did an extra special job cleaning around my desk and disinfected my chair. The next day I was surprised that my hives had disappeared. I later figured out that the chair itself hadn't been cleaned in a long time, and something about it was creating an allergic reaction. A little bit of help from a cleaning person saved my sanity and sure made life a lot easier."

If employees are suffering from allergies, professional cleaners can take extra care to clean up any possible allergens in their environment. This might include cleaning out air conditioning ducts – which are prime sources of dust – disinfecting surfaces, and deep cleaning carpets in the area.

EMPLOYEE MORALE IS IMPROVED

Believe it or not, the cleanliness and organization of the workplace can have a dramatic effect on the morale of employees. An office that is cleaned regularly signals into your team that you are committed to providing them a good place to work and that you care about their environment.

Think of maintaining a clean space as a signal that you deliver a safe and tidy environment to everyone on the team.

Most people enjoy working in an uncluttered and well-kept environment. This gives employees a sense of pride in their office or workspace and makes them more likely to enjoy being part of the group.

Clean environments reduce illnesses and health problems, relieve stress, improve productivity, and reduce allergic reactions. All these things work together to heighten the morale of your team.

Hazards of Not Cleaning

The hazards of an unclean business largely depend on the type of business. For instance, businesses that serve the public directly, such as restaurants, must be kept to a high standard of cleanliness because there are hazards associated with the preparation, storage and disposal of food.

Spoiled food in a restaurant can attract insects, rodents and other pests. This can lead to diseases and public relations nightmares when diners discover cockroaches in their salads. Governments generally inspect restaurants for cleanliness, and failures can cause diners to find other places to eat or even can shut down a business.

On the other hand, a back office not frequented by the public may not need to maintain as high a standard because the risks are significantly less. This doesn't imply that those offices shouldn't be clean – quite the contrary. But the type of hazards as well as the risks are different.

Let's look at some of the hazards and risks of not cleaning.

HEALTH

There are microorganisms all around us all the time. Bacteria live on our skin, in our bodies, and are present on every surface on the planet. Even hospitals, which you would think must be kept meticulously clean, are filled with bacteria, some harmless and some dangerous.

That being said, cleaning reduces the incidence of bacteria and other pests that can cause us harm.

A friend of mine reported on his recent vacation experience, "I was driving on a road trip a few weeks ago, and I had to stop at a gas station. I was horrified at the state of the restrooms. The word nasty doesn't even come close to describing the condition. There was no way that I was going to expose myself and my family to filth and diseases by using their facilities. We found a much cleaner facility a few miles down the road, and they got our business."

As you can see, not only was did this restroom potentially expose patrons to health hazards, it resulted in a loss of business for the gas station. A nasty restroom directly affected the bottom line of that company.

Restrooms in any business are a prime source of disease and must be cleaned frequently using the appropriate techniques and chemicals. A quick cleaning is not enough; a thorough scrubbing is required to keep your staff healthy and reduce the spread of illnesses such as the flu and colds.

Many businesses provide kitchens, and because these contain food and garbage they are breeding grounds for disease. Ensuring the dishes are washed, the refrigerators are cleaned, and surfaces are wiped down with bacteria killing chemicals will help keep your staff healthy.

Trash cans are often filled with uneaten food and other waste materials that degrade and serve as breeding grounds for rodents and other pests, as well as bacteria. Those must be emptied daily as part of a cleaning regimen.

Many people suffer from allergies to dust and other environmental hazards. Allergies can be minor, resulting in a mild headache or swelling, to severe resulting in life-threatening situations.

Dust built up in air ducts can blow down on employees from overhead vents. Over time, this can cause a variety of symptoms that can be difficult to diagnose. These allergies can cause symptoms that appear to be the same as colds or flu's including rashes, headaches, joint aches and can even make conditions such as asthma worse.

Contaminated air contains millions of tiny dust mites, which are insects that thrive in dirty conditions. These mites are the cause of many different types of allergies.

Recently, I talked with someone about their allergies at work, "I couldn't figure out why I was having such problems with my breathing all the time. It was becoming a real problem, and I felt like I was going crazy. One day I'd feel fine in the next I was gasping for breath throughout the afternoon. I was getting desperate, and then I realized that my allergies got worse every time it was hot outside; the heat kicked in the air conditioning, which stirred up the dust that had accumulated in the air vents. My employer was kind enough to call in a cleaning service to clean out the ductwork, and I haven't had a severe allergy attack since."

These allergies reduce the productivity of your employees because people find it more difficult to work when they don't feel well. Because the symptoms can often appear to be severe, your employees may take more sick days, or be irritable due to lack of sleep.

Employees that discover that they are having allergic reactions to conditions in the workplace are subject to ADA protection and might even be able to take legal action.

FIRE

The storage of paper, cardboard, wood, chemicals and other flammable materials brings with it the risk of fire.

Business's commonly don't consider the risks of storing boxes of old reports or forms in their building. Paper is flammable, especially when the humidity is low.

"We had to do an audit," an office manager told me recently, "and our accounting department recalled over a thousand boxes of forms and other papers from storage. We stacked hundreds of these boxes along the walls all around the accounting office, and in closets, and even filled up two conference rooms."

The problem can be even worse if paper supplies are stored in the same place as flammable chemicals such as paints or solvents. You'll often see this in closets and storage rooms. Half-filled paint cans, cleaning supplies, solvents, and even fertilizers are flammable or explosive and can cause disasters to occur in your office.

Another thing that I commonly see when I visit offices for the first time is old building supplies such as scrap lumber and sawdust stacked behind an office or to the side of the patio. When these materials are located next to a smoking area, on a hot, dry day they can be disasters waiting to happen.

"We didn't have a cleaning company," an employee told me. "Instead, employees were responsible for cleaning their own areas and emptying their own trash. As you can guess, quite often this was forgotten in the rush of getting things done. One day, one of the trash cans caught on fire. We weren't sure why; perhaps somebody was smoking when they shouldn't have been. By the time we were able to get a fire extinguisher, the entire desk was aflame. We did manage to put it out before it spread any further, but it was close. Another 30 seconds and the whole office would have been engulfed in flames."

CODE VIOLATIONS

Many buildings are inspected by government agencies to verify compliance with various codes and regulations. This is to ensure the safety of customers, (as in the case of a restaurant), workers and the surrounding area.

Fire inspectors visit virtually all office buildings on at least a yearly basis to ensure there are no flammable hazards such as exposed wiring, incorrectly installed stoves in a kitchen, and so forth.

A computer technician told me, "we had our yearly fire inspection and I thought it was going to go fine because in previous years they just quickly walked through the place, made a few notes, and left without saying anything. However, this time they noticed that our office was unusually messy, and they decided to take a closer look. They found that the wiring under our computer room didn't meet code, which resulted in some very expensive retrofits. I suppose it's a good thing that they found the problem, but the lack of cleanliness was a clue for them to take a closer look."

Building inspectors generally see unclean or trashy areas as a warning sign that there may be deeper problems that need to be addressed.

Fire inspectors prefer to see office spaces that are clean and tidy. If they see unkempt areas, papers piled to the ceiling, trash cans not emptied, and other nonoptimal things, they may decide to take a closer look. You'll get code violations for any problems they find, and they'll demand that you fix them along with giving you a fine. Some businesses can even be closed if the violations are severe.

FINANCIAL

An unclean office environment can have a direct and indirect effect on the finances of your business.

Spills that are not cleaned up can cause slip and fall accidents which can send an employee onto disability and even result in lawsuits.

Germs and infections originating in dirty bathrooms, filthy kitchens, and, believe it or not, cell phones can make the members of your team sick, which results in lost productivity and drop morale.

"It seems that every few months," an office manager mentioned to me during our initial consultation, "a plague – respiratory problems – affects high proportion of the staff. Half the office seems to be coughing, and the other half are taking shortened days or using sick time."

After a thorough cleaning by a professional cleaning staff, her team almost magically began to feel better. Since she began cleaning regularly, the "plague" vanished, never to be seen again.

Customers who visit your office may be discouraged if they find unclean working conditions, because that is often equated with poor service and the lack of integrity.

A frustrated businessman explained his problem to me, "customers come into my office to talk about doing business, and for some reason many of them decided to go with a competitor. A few days ago, I got extremely frustrated because I was sure I had nailed some business but they decided to go elsewhere. I picked up the phone and asked her what was going on. After some hesitation because she didn't want to hurt my feelings, she mentioned that the junkiness in my office discouraged her. That's why I called you. I had no idea that a little clutter was costing me money. In fact, the amount that I lost from that one sale would have paid for a cleaning crew for years."

CONCLUSIONS

The hazards of an unclean office environment are very real but are often not obvious. Clutter causes lost productivity, spills cause slip and fall accidents, dust causes allergies, filth causes disease and illness, and papers and chemicals can cause fires.

What amazes many business people is the fact that cluttered and filthy offices results in lost business opportunities. Customers are not impressed by businesses that don't have the integrity to keep their own space clean and tidy.

I know it often seems like hiring a professional cleaning company is optional and doesn't have that big of an effect. However, the hazards of not cleaning are very real, and the benefits are tremendous.

Hazards of Cleaning

Let's look at cleaning from a different point of view. Are there hazards and dangers that cleaning people face while they're performing cleaning tasks? (Five Hazards of Professional Cleaning, 2016)

CHEMICALS

All types of cleaning products that contain chemicals have inherent dangers. The ingredients can cause health problems, be highly flammable, corrosive, or lead to burns, allergies, and other symptoms.

Many of these products contain chemicals that can cause irritation in the eyes, throat and skin. They can also cause headaches, stomach aches, diarrhea and other troubling symptoms. Even the most innocent seeming products that contain citrus or are so-called "green" can have side effects running from irritating to life-threatening (Organic Consumers Association).

The chemicals used in cleaning, even green chemicals, can be toxic to the human body, and can be life-threatening if there is skin contact or they are inhaled.

Think about all the products used to clean and office:

- ammonia
- natural pH cleaner
- degreasers
- spot cleaners
- cleansers
- disinfectants
- detergent
- solvents
- Chlorine bleach

Each of these comes with the potential for causing harm to people, animals, and the environment.

It's important to choose cleaning products that do not contain or have reduced amounts of VOCs (volatile organic compounds), irritants, flammable materials and fragrances. Since your cleaning crew will be using these chemicals day in and day out for hours at a time, you'll want to reduce their exposure to anything that might harm them. Additionally, residues can cause allergic reactions hours or even days after the chemicals are applied.

Some tips about cleaning with chemicals include (CCOHS):

- Read the instructions and make sure you understand them.
- Read the safety data sheet, if one is available, so you understand any potential hazards.
- Where the appropriate protective clothing such as gloves, goggles and so forth as needed.
- Perform any vacuuming, grooming, or other cleaning before you use the chemicals.
- After cleaning, even if you're wearing gloves, wash your hands thoroughly with soap and rinse with water.

Things you should not do while cleaning with chemicals include:

- Don't eat while you're using any kind of cleaning chemical.

- Don't drink anything while cleaning with chemicals.
- Do not smoke.
- Don't leave open containers of chemicals sitting around where other people can run into them.
- Don't mix chemicals together. This is especially true of products which contain chlorine and ammonia, which combined can cause injuries and even death.

Some of the kinds of chemicals that you can run into while cleaning include:

- **Asbestos**, which is a fibrous material that used to be used for insulation. It can still be found in older buildings, and has been demonstrated to cause problems with breathing, lung cancer, and mesothelioma.
- Corrosive materials such as acid.
- Flammable liquids.
- Metalworking fluids.
- Pesticides.
- Compressed gases.

- Explosive gases.
- And many others.

Professional cleaners are trained to deal with any kinds of chemicals or materials they may find in a safe manner.

Respect your chemicals and understand that they can be dangerous if misused. However, with proper training, or even just reading the instructions, cleaning with chemicals is fine.

PHYSICAL DANGERS

Cleaning crews are exposed to many different dangers of a physical nature. They often move furniture a regular basis, stand on ladders or chairs to clean high places, and pick up heavy items. Slippery floors lead to slip and fall accidents, and exposed items can cause trip and fall accidents.

The work equipment comes with its own set of cautions, including electrical hazards and injuries from spinning or rapidly moving equipment.

Air Quality

Anytime you clean, a host of chemicals and particles are thrown up into the air. Even the simple act of dusting or vacuuming can cause immense air pollution inside an office.

Dust contains small amount of pollen from plants, hairs, bits of paper, dirt, skin cells, harsh chemicals, soot, carpet fluff, and excrement. On top of that, small creatures called dust mites (very tiny relatives of spiders) feed off dust and human skin.

Each time you walk, puffs of dust are thrown up from the carpet into the air. Every time you pull a book off a shelf some dust is released into the environment. Dust is everywhere, and it can't be avoided without heavy filtration.

As part of their job, cleaning crews do stir up a lot of dust. Most of this settles down within a few hours back into the carpets and onto shelves where it is more or less harmless.

Cleaning crews, however, constantly work in the middle of clouds of dust, breathing in those tiny particles for hours each day.

Dust can cause health issues from minor allergies up to life-threatening breathing problems.

Cleaning crews are trained in the proper procedures to reduce their exposure to dust by wearing masks, gloves and other protective gear.

BIOLOGICAL HAZARDS

As you clean you may be exposed to infectious pathogens, mold spores, fungi and bacteria. The obvious places to be exposed to these dangers is the restroom and kitchen, but biological hazards exist in all phases of cleaning.

Think about what people bring into a building on the bottom of their shoes, and you'll understand what I mean by this. That debris is carried into buildings, scraped on floors, and ground into carpets.

Cleaning crews are trained in dealing with biological hazards and where the appropriate protection for their hands, lungs and even their skin to protect themselves as needed.

Cleaning any bodily fluids such as blood, ensure you follow safety procedures:

- Wear gloves.
- Use disposable towels, brooms, mops, shovels or something else to keep from touching the fluid itself.
- Disinfect any equipment that was used to clean the fluids.
- Any soil cleaning materials are considered hazardous biologicals and should be disposed of in a leakproof plastic bag.
- Use gloves are considered contaminated and should also be disposed of.
- Most important of all, make sure that you do not come in direct contact with any bodily fluids.

CONCLUSIONS

On the surface, it often seems that cleaning is something that can be done by amateurs. After all, how hard can it be? Run a vacuum, wipe down some windows, scrub the restroom, and so forth. What's hazardous about all that?

It's important to understand that janitorial services are considered one of the most dangerous jobs that can be performed (Charpentier). Cleaning crews are exposed to chemicals, biological agents, and physical hazards every time they do their job.

That's a great reason to hire a professional cleaning company. They are obligated to train their personnel to reduce accidents, limit exposure to harsh chemicals, and handle any kind of biological hazards.

Wouldn't you rather your cleaning be done by professionals who are trained in the requisite safety procedures?

Areas to Be Cleaned

Start your employees on the right foot every day by ensuring that they walk into clean working facilities. They will be more productive, have higher morale, and will have less illnesses than they would in unclean offices. Healthy and happy employees help the bottom line of your company.

Let's look at each of the different areas in a typical office so you can gain a better understanding of what needs to be cleaned, why, and the benefits involved.

THE PARKING LOT, WINDOWS AND WALLS
Many cleaning companies don't deal with parking lots and the outer walls and windows of your building. Nonetheless, the first thing your customers see is the state of the parking lot, your windows, doors, and walls.

Parking lots covered with leaves and other debris can result in injuries due to slip and falls, and that can lead to lawsuits and lost productivity. This is especially true after a rainfall, which can in turn change covered parking lots into virtual death traps.

Additionally, a buildup of grime, leaves, garbage, and other debris gives an immediate bad impression to your customers and vendors. This kind of trash degrades over time, which can introduce some foul smells and unsightly views.

On top of that, graffiti covered walls give the impression of an unsafe area due to potential gang or criminal activity. Graffiti should be painted over immediately because it can result in lost business.

Grimy windows, dirty walls, and filthy doors give visitors a very bad impression of the health and morale of your business.

Don't forget about the area behind and beside your business as well, especially if you have entranceways in the back or it's possible for customers to get into those areas. Clean up any old construction material, cans of paint, and other debris, and ensure the weeds are kept to a reasonable level. There been many occasions when I've gone out of the back or side door to a business to discover piles of trash and debris.

LOBBY

One of the most important places on which to focus your cleaning is your lobby, foyer or reception area. This is the first place inside your building that seen by your customers, and it's important to create a great first impression. This helps win over the confidence of potential clients. An unclean lobby gives a poor first impression and can even, if it's bad enough, lose business.

The focus should be on ensuring the windows are clean, any plants (real or fake) have been dusted, the carpets are vacuumed, floors are mopped or swept up at least, and the counters are wiped clean and free from any clutter.

Don't forget to dust and wipe down any knickknacks and artwork in the lobby area. Also, wipe clean the glass on any paintings or posters occasionally. You'd be surprised how these services attract fingerprints and dust.

RESTROOMS

You can bet that many of your clients are going to ask to use your restroom, especially after a long drive or a lunch meeting. Obviously, employees and other visitors will also use the facilities regularly.

The cleanliness of your restrooms will make an impression on your clients – keep them clean to make sure it's a good one. Dirty bathrooms can become very unpleasant very quickly.

Restrooms are also breeding grounds for diseases and can cause illnesses among your staff and visitors. They should be scrub down daily either before you open the office or after it's closed.

Don't forget to restock toiletries regularly for obvious reasons.

LUNCH ROOM

Many offices have lunchrooms or even cafeterias depending on their size. Because these are often not visited by customers, they tend to get less care than other areas. Other than washing the dishes, many office kitchens don't receive regular cleanings at all.

Unfortunately, dirty kitchens are hazardous to the health of your employees. Diseases and germs grow in sinks and refrigerators, and on shelves and countertops. These environments can be detrimental to the health and well-being of your employees.

Ensure sinks and countertops are scrubbed regularly – daily if possible – with antibacterial cleaners. Anywhere water can accumulate should also be addressed at the same time. If you see any leaks, get them fixed immediately. Small pools of standing water can become putrid with disease quickly.

Keep the lunchroom free from clutter, and regularly inspect the contents of refrigerators and shelves. Throw away any outdated or old food, and obviously anything that turned green or has begun to smell.

Clean lunchrooms improve the morale and health of your workforce.

Conference Rooms

I'm always amazed by how many conference rooms seem to double as storage facilities. Often, I'll find boxes of yellowed and barely legible reports dating back years if not decades, stored in crumbling boxes lining the walls.

Remember, conference rooms are used by your staff, clients and vendors on a regular basis. They should be free from clutter, and not used as extra storage space. Obviously, any trashcans should be emptied.

Wipe down any tables, and don't forget to disinfect the chairs and phones, including the speakerphone.

Offices

Your employees spend most of their time in their offices or in their cubicles. Clutter accumulates on top of their desk, on any shelves, and on filing cabinets. Often, their trashcan will be filled with a variety of garbage, including food, papers, boxes, equipment, and just about anything else you can imagine.

Many companies will allow employees to eat at their desks, which can lead to a wide variety of food related trash. Greasy pizza boxes and Chinese food containers are common. The problem is these debris contain food particles which can attract insects and other pests.

Pick up any trash, into the trashcan's, wipe off the desks and shelves, and tidy things up. Ensure that the carpets around all desks are regularly vacuumed and shampooed on a regular basis.

PHONES

Office phones are perhaps one of the dirtiest possessions and are covered in bacteria. It is likely that a phone has more germs than a toilet seat. (Abrams, 2017)

According to The Health Site (The Health Site, 2015), these objects are cleaner than your phone.

- A public toilet
- The soles of your shoes
- Your pet's eating dish

- Kitchen counters
- Door knows
- A bundle of notes

Even worse, studies have found that many phones have bacteria containing E. coli, which is a germ that can lead to infections. These can cause emphysema, MRSA, diarrhea, cramps, and vomiting, as well as a host of other symptoms.

Think about it; people use phones after eating, after using restrooms, while sweating, and after a host of other activities. All these past germs from the human body to all parts of the phone.

What do you do about it? Phones must be cleaned with antibacterial agents such as alcohol regularly. I recommend they be cleaned every day. (Singh, 2014)

If you do nothing else to stay healthy, regularly clean your phones – both the one in your office and the one in your pocket. Also, if you use someone else's phone, you might want to use an antibacterial wipe before placing it close to your mouth.

CLOSETS AND SUPPLY ROOMS

Many businesses forget to clean their closets, supply cabinets and supply rooms. After all, these are usually closed and off-limits to the public.

These need to be cleaned for several reasons:

- Any food or other supplies can go out of date, and those need to be inspected and tossed if necessary.
- Ensure your supplies are stored in a neat and tidy manner to make it easy to get to them when you need them.
- Cleaning helps prevent the incidence of pests such as insects and rodents.
- When you clean, you're also inspecting, so keep your eyes open for signs of water leakage, damage, rodents, and other undesirable things.
- People tend to just throw things into supply closets and rooms, which causes them to fill up very quickly. As you

clean, all that junk can be inspected, tidied up or thrown out if needed.

Perceptions

The fact of the matter is that a clean environment is more productive then a dirty environment. Getting work done in a messy office can be challenging or nearly impossible.

As you sit there at your desk, your eyes often wander over the clutter, and this can keep you from concentrating on getting your job done. Unclean environments can also cause an increase in employee illnesses and allergies and reduce the respect of your customers for your brand and your company.

What does a cleaning company do for you?

THE FRONT OF THE BUILDING

Imagine you are a customer. You've traveled for an hour through traffic to get to the offices of a business. Your tired, slightly grumpy from the long drive in the heat, and you need to use the restroom.

The parking lot is almost full, but eventually you find a space under a tree relatively close to the front door. As you step out of the car, you're clean, expensive shoes sink into a pile of decaying leaves, dirt and other filth. It appears the trash and debris has been accumulating for quite some time.

You shake your head in disgust, thinking "they can't even keep their parking lot clean?"

Walking towards the front door, you see that the windows facing the parking lot are covered in grime. As you come closer, you notice a spiderweb in the upper left corner. The spider stares back at you as if daring you to enter its abode.

You shrug and think "maybe they're so busy working on important contracts that they just don't have time to clean. Maybe this is a good sign."

You haven't even entered the building yet, and the lack of cleanliness is already making a bad impression.

Reception Areas

Pushing open the front doors, you enter the lobby and quickly walk up to the reception desk. The receptionist smiles at you, and you tell her the name of the person that you're here to see. She makes a quick call and asks you to make yourself comfortable.

As you sit on the couch, a cloud of dust envelops you. This causes you to cough uncontrollably for a minute, and you ask the receptionist if she has any water. She disappears from moment and returns with a bottle which she hands to you with a smile.

Taking a drink from the bottle comforts your throat and stops the coughing. You put your hand down on the armrest of the chair, then notice that it feels a bit sticky. Taking a closer look, you can see that sometime in the past someone spilled soda or something that was never cleaned up.

You want to wash off the stickiness, and you are reminded that you need to visit the restroom anyway. The receptionist tells you it's just down the hall.

THE RESTROOM

Getting to the restroom turns out to be a little more challenging than you would've expected. Boxes of old accounting records are stacked to the ceiling on each side of the hall, making it a tight squeeze to get through.

After a few minutes, you reach the door of the restroom, feeling slightly annoyed.

Once you step inside, you wrinkle your nose in disgust.

"Don't they ever clean this thing? What a mess!"

It's not the worst restroom you've ever seen – that one you stopped at in the desert on the way to Barstow was just plain nasty – but it's still not a pretty sight.

THE CONFERENCE ROOM

After working your way back to the lobby, you sat back down in the chair, being careful not to touch the sticky armrest. A few minutes later, the receptionist announces that she'll show you to a conference room you'll be meeting with the person you came to see.

Walking behind her, you noticed that the carpets are a bit threadbare and worn in places with a few stains here and there. It's not exactly filthy, it just looks well used and appears to not have been cleaned recently.

You reach the conference room, shake hands with your appointment, and sit down in a chair. You notice an overflowing wastebasket in one corner, and see the windows haven't been cleaned in quite a while. That's a shame, because the view of the garden outside would be improved if the glass wasn't covered in dirt.

OFFICE SPACE

Once your meeting is over, your appointment shows you the way out. As he guides you through various desks in the open office environment, you notice that there's a general appearance of disarray. Trash cans aren't emptied, there are a few boxes of half eaten pizza piled up in a corner, and there are a couple of stains in the carpet.

THOUGHTS ABOUT AN UNCLEAN OFFICE

This was a guided tour of a typical office that hasn't engaged with a cleaning service. The business is depending on employees or cheap contracted help to do the cleaning, and they are obviously not doing a very good job of it.

How would visiting this office make you feel? Would you want to do business with them? Or does it give you a sense of unease about the quality of work that you'll receive?

If they can't even keep their own office clean, how can they be expected to do a good job?

Customer perception is everything, and first impressions can never be repeated. That first look at your office will create a picture in the mind of your customer that lasts forever.

Obviously, an unclean or cluttered office doesn't necessarily mean you're going to lose business or that customers are going to run away from you as fast as they can.

But the lack of cleanliness does degrade the impression created in the mind of your customers about your business. Your cleanliness, or lack of it, can be viewed as incompetence.

Competent people tend to keep their work areas relatively clean.

Competent companies and businesses should take the same attitude.

Your customers, vendors and employees form an impression of you and your business based on many different factors. The cleanliness of your office space is one of their considerations; obviously, price, quality, speed of delivery, and other variables also fit into the picture.

But since it is so easy to maintain cleanliness, why not eliminate any doubt in that area in the minds of your customers?

All you need to do is hire a competent cleaning service, who will perform their duties regularly to keep your space clean and looking good.

And if your offices look good, then your business looks good on first impression.

As I said earlier, you only get one chance to make a first impression. Why not make sure it's a good one?

Floors

When you walk into a building, one of the first things you see is the floor.

What do you think when you see a business with dirty, dull or dingy floors?

I remember walking into a supermarket in my local area and noticing that the floors look terrible. The finish was dingy as if it hadn't been cleaned in a while, and there was noticeable dirt in the corners and edges near the shelving. Additionally, there were scuff marks as if someone had dragged equipment across the room.

Guess what? I found a different place to shop. A dingy and dirty floor meant to me that supermarket was not well maintained and perhaps even a health risk. I found a store, slightly further away, that went to the trouble of keeping its floors, and the rest of the store of course, clean.

When you think about cleaning, floors are of supreme importance. That's because dirt, dust, spills, and grime fall or floats from furniture and other places downward to your concrete, tile, hardwood or carpeted floors.

But don't think it's just a matter of mopping or sweeping occasionally. Each floor is different and requires different chemicals and techniques to ensure they are not damaged and that they are cleaned properly. For example, concrete floors absorb liquids, so must be dried quickly. Different types of carpets must be shampooed or cleaned with different chemicals, machines, and even water temperatures.

Your professional cleaning crew will do a thorough job of vacuuming and mopping your floors. They have also been trained to understand what techniques, equipment and supplies are required for each type of flooring.

FLOOR DEBRIS

Think about it – every time you put something on a shelf, you stir up dust, which floats downward and some of it winds up on the floor.

People walk on the floor, leaving scuff marks, dirt, and debris that the hall in from outside. Everything that gets picked up on people's shoes winds up on the floor in one form or another. When you think about what winds up on the bottom of your shoe, you can understand why floors need to be cleaned often.

Drinks and other liquids are spilt on carpet and any other floor surface, leaving stains or causing damage if not quickly and properly cleaned up.

In the kitchen, garbage, half eaten food, crumbs, and other waste products fall to the floor and are often not picked up and put into the trash. This debris attracts insects, pests, and can cause damage to carpets and tile.

In restaurants, overflowing sinks and toilets can cause foul and germ ridden water and its contents to spill on the floor. If not properly cleaned up, this toxic water can lead to illnesses, foul smells, and damage.

Water and other liquids spilt on floors can result in lawsuits from slip and fall accidents.

Additionally, these liquids can damage flooring and carpets. This is especially true of hardwood and porous tile flooring.

WHY CLEAN THE FLOORS?

Now, think about what happens is people move around on the floor.

When someone walks on carpet, any dust, dust mites, tiny woodchips, paper particles, bits of food, and everything else gets thrown up into the air for people to breathe, get on their hands, and even get into their mouths.

People with allergies are particularly vulnerable to dust, dust mites, and all the other tiny particles thrown up into the air. It may not be obvious that the allergies are caused by dirty floors and carpets, which makes them difficult to diagnose.

Debris get ground into carpets and floors every time they are stepped on. All the dirt and garbage that winds up on the bottom of your shoe gets mashed into carpets, concrete flooring, and porous tile. The more the floors are walked on, the more difficult it is to clean because the debris is forced deep into pores or the fiber of carpets.

There are several types of floors in commercial buildings. Each of these types of floors requires a different schedule and type of cleaning.

Insects and pests of all types are tiny enough that they can find small bits of food and garbage left anywhere in your office. The crumbs from that pizza that your crew ate because they work late will be found and eaten by cockroaches, mice, and other pests.

All this debris slowly decays as it sits on your floor. This decay can produce smells that are difficult to locate and can attract even more insect and other pests.

On top of this, some of this debris and garbage causes damage to certain types of floors. Hardwood floors can be damaged by spills and other materials if they are not regularly cleaned. For example, gritty materials, such as sand, can grind through the waterproof coating on most hardwood floors to cause permanent damage requiring expensive fixes.

For these and many other reasons, vacuuming, mopping and cleaning of floors is an essential daily, or almost daily, requirement.

There are several different kinds of floors that are common in office environments.

FLOOR CLEANING EQUIPMENT
Your professional cleaner uses many kinds of equipment to clean floors. (B-Air, 2017)

- A bucket to hold water and chemicals.
- Cleaners of various types. The chemicals that are used will depend upon the requirements of the customer and the type of floor being cleaned.
- Water. Believe it or not, water is an excellent cleaner all by itself.
- A mop or two.
- A soft bristled broom.
- A vacuum cleaner.
- A power buffing machine.
- A floor drying fan.

- Floor finish.

Each different kind of floor, discussed in the following sections, requires specialized equipment and supplies to do the optimum job. Choosing the wrong chemical or tool can do more harm than good.

COMMERCIAL TILE FLOORS

Vinyl composition tile floors, also called VCT, is one of the most common choices for commercial builders. These are formed into a solid sheet and cut to fit a room.

VCT flooring is often used in high traffic areas in offices because it's inexpensive and easy to maintain.

This type of floor requires a neutral cleaner with the pH of seven. First, the floors swept or vacuumed, and then it is scrubbed with detergent. Optionally, the floor may be dried with an air mover for at least 30 minutes.

A neutral cleaner must be used because the wrong chemical can make the floor appear to be grimy and strip off the finish.

COMMERCIAL CONCRETE FLOORS

Some buildings use commercial concrete floors because they are very durable, can withstand large amounts of traffic, are resistant to stains and damage, and are easy to maintain. (MediaBeast, 2017)

Concrete is easy to clean. The flooring is vacuumed or swept, then mopped using a clean mop and neutral floor cleaner.

Once the floor has been mopped, it's important to dry it quickly because liquids are absorbed into the flooring. This occurs even if the floor is sealed.

Any particles remaining on the floor act as sand paper, which over time will cause damage and make the floor look worn and dull. It's important to perform regular sweeping and mopping to make concrete floors last as long as possible.

COMMERCIAL CARPET FLOORS

Since businesses often have higher traffic than residential homes, more rugged carpeting is required. Commercial grade carpets are made from nylon or olefin (polypropylene). Nylon is the most durable fiber and tends to last longer.

Carpeted floors should be vacuumed every time your professional cleaner visits to help them last longer and to clean up any dust or grime that has accumulated. Monthly, quarterly or even yearly, the carpet needs to be cleaned with professional shampooing equipment.

COMMERCIAL VINYL FLOORS

Many businesses use vinyl flooring for high-traffic areas because it resists water, comes in a large variety of patterns, and is easy to clean.

For commercial vinyl floors, sweep or vacuum the floor to remove any large debris, then mop it with a neutral floor cleaning detergent. An air mover can optionally be used to dry the floor quickly.

Regular mopping, sweeping and vacuuming keeps dust and small particles from accumulating on the floor and causing damage. These particles have sharp edges, and act much like sandpaper.

COMMERCIAL HARDWOOD FLOORS

For areas such as lobbies that get high-traffic yet also must look good, commercial Hardwood floors are an excellent choice. These are resistant to spills and damage, but they tend to require more maintenance than other forms of flooring.

Hardwood has a porous surface, and dirt can get deeply embedded in it. It's best to put a protective sealant over the wood to help it last longer. Regular mopping with a liquid cleaner (using the manufacturer's recommendation) will keep your floor clean.

Begin by using a dust mop to handle any particles that might scratch or damage the floor. After that, use a damp mop (but not saturated) with the appropriate chemical cleaner (as recommended by the manufacturer) to thoroughly mop the floor. An air mover can be used to dry the floors quickly.

Of course, on all these types of floors, any spills need to be cleaned up and any damage must be repaired immediately. Taking these steps will cause your floors to last longer and look better.

How to Clean

As we've already established in this book, a business with a clean workspace is more appealing to employees and customers then a filthy mess. The morale of workers is increased by a clean environment, and clients receive a much better impression of you and your business.

When your office is clean by professional cleaning company, what do they do? Do they use some mysterious magic, secret formulas or special techniques handed down for generations?

Cleaning is best done by professionals because they know how to clean anything. Team members have been trained for everything from the mundane task of sweeping up the floor to more specialized things such as removing specific kinds of stains from carpets or handling hazardous materials.

Professional cleaners receive regular training, so they understand what to do with any cleaning or decluttering situation. They take new courses, and retake old courses regularly to constantly update themselves on new techniques, chemicals, machinery, and other things that have changed about the best way to clean and environment.

STEPS OF CLEANING

Cleaning is best done in specific steps and in a certain order to optimize the amount of time it takes to get the whole job done. For example, dusting of cabinets should be done before vacuuming so that the dust can be vacuumed off the floor after it has been stirred up. Waiting until after vacuuming to do the dusting leaves the dust in the carpets.

In the same way, mopping the floor is one of the last steps of cleaning because dirt and grime tend to fall down to the floor. You want to wait until it is all accumulated before you mop it up. If you do the mopping first, then you leave the floors dirty.

CLEAN UP LOOSE PAPERS

One of the first things a cleaning crew will do is organize loose papers and documents.

Papers that are scattered over the tops of desks, on the floor, or sitting on top of file cabinets are messy and it can be time-consuming to find specific items when needed.

The cleaning staff will use caution when moving around papers, since those can be placed specific areas by individuals with a unique "filing system". Generally, papers are simply stacked in neat piles on the desk where they came from or moved to the top of cabinets or tables.

Your professional cleaning crew does not normally file papers away in file cabinets since they don't have any way to understand where things should go, what is important, and what is confidential.

DUST

One of the primary tasks of your cleaning crew is to dust any shelves, countertops, plants (real or artificial), paintings or other things hanging on the wall, the tops of file cabinets, and so forth.

As previously mentioned, dusting is generally done first because the dust will move from the tops of cabinets and bookshelves to the floor, where it can be vacuumed or mopped up later.

WIPE DOWN FURNITURE
Once dusting has been done, any countertops desktops, or other horizontal surfaces will get wiped down losing mild cleaning solutions or even water.

WASTE BASKETS
It should be obvious that wastebaskets will be emptied during every cleaning. It's recommended that you line your wastebaskets with plastic bags so that any spills or messes don't leak out of the trashcan.

It's important that garbage be placed in waste baskets because your cleaners won't throw anything away unless it's clearly garbage and belongs in the trash. This is important, because obviously you don't want useful items or important papers thrown away accidentally.

But anything in a trashcan or wastebasket is fair game for the cleaners to throw out.

CLEAN THE BATHROOMS

The bathrooms must be cleaned regularly; in fact, they should be cleaned several times a day. Each time your cleaning crew comes then, they will thoroughly disinfect and scrub down your restrooms. This is necessary for a clean office as well as the health and safety of employee's, vendors and customers.

- Toilet bowls are scrubbed with a disinfectant and brush. The seat, lid, the bowl, the tank and the base are disinfected.
- The floors are swept and mopped with a disinfectant.
- Toilet tissue roles, including some extras, are replaced or refilled.
- Soap dispensers refilled.
- Paper towel holders are also refilled.
- The sink and countertops are disinfected.
- The doorknob and the surrounding area, both inside and outside, are also disinfected because those are touched by everyone.
- Mirrors are cleaned.

As you can see, restrooms are quite thoroughly cleaned because they are a source of germs and infections.

Thoroughly clean restrooms result in a healthier staff and give your customers a better impression of your business.

If you don't clean your restrooms regularly, you can count on a greater rate of illnesses among your staff, and your customers will leave your office with negative feelings about your business.

CLEANING DEVICES

Professional cleaners understand they need to be careful when cleaning electronic and other devices. Some cleaners can damage electronics or screens, and others are not effective.

- Television screens and monitors should be turned off and allowed to cool down before cleaning.
- Before cleaning, the display needs to be dusted to remove any grit or dirt. If this is not done, scratches may result.

- Once the dusting is done, your cleaner will wipe down the screen with the soft, lint free cloth. This removes any remaining dust.
- Next, they'll use an alcohol and water preparation, 50% of each, to clean off the screen. The lint free cloth should be damp but not saturated, and the screen should be gently wiped.
- After that, they'll use a dry, lint free cloth to clean off any excess moisture. Make sure any moisture is drive before turning the monitor or television back on.

Your professional cleaner will never use paper towels to clean your display, because that results in small bits of paper being left on the screen.

Windex and other glass cleaners containing ammonia can damage your screen. Stay away from those.

Only isopropyl alcohol or water is used for screen cleaning. Do not use ethyl alcohol, Ethel acid, ammonia, methyl chloride, or other chemicals.

THE BREAK ROOM, KITCHEN OR CAFETERIA

Cleaning the kitchen area or, and larger organizations, the cafeteria is essential to keep your employees healthy and safe.

- The refrigerator will be cleaned and organized by a professional cleaner. Any old food (if it can be identified as old) will be thrown out and the interior will be wiped down with disinfectant.
- Some companies have a company policy that all food is to be thrown out at the end of the week regardless of its condition. This makes it easier for your professional cleaner to know what goes in the trash and what doesn't.
- The inside and outside of the microwave will be cleaned with a disinfectant rag.
- Any dishes will be washed.
- The sink will be cleaned with a disinfectant.
- Counters will be wiped down with a disinfectant.
- Hand and dishtowels will be washed.

- If you have dish sponges, they will be replaced regularly, although not every time.

Professional planners understand the purpose of each chemical used in cleaning and are trained in the risks and benefits of each one.

Disinfectant, cleansers and other chemicals are used to provide the maximum amount of cleanliness for each situation found in office. All these chemicals are harmful in one way or another. These can cause anything from minor irritation of the skin all the way up to life-threatening situations.

Professional cleaning companies take the appropriate precautions to ensure its staff is trained to handle any chemicals using proper and safe procedures.

Commonly used chemicals include:

- Water, which is a very powerful cleaning agent. Water is an excellent solvent and can be used safely in most situations.
- Soap or detergent.

- Ammonia.
- Powdered bleach or calcium hypochlorite.
- Citric acid.
- Liquid bleach or sodium hypochlorite.
- Sodium hydroxide, also known as lie.
- Vinegar or acetic acid.
- And many others.

A few cleaning agents are described below. There are many others, and these are just some of the more common ones.

Acidic cleaning agents such as vinegar, hydrochloric acid, sulfuric acid and so forth are used to remove inorganic deposits, greases, proteins and other materials.

Alkaline cleaning agents include sodium hydroxide, potassium hydroxide, bleach and ammonia. These are used to dissolve fats, grease, oils and other protein-based materials.

Degreasers are cleaning agents that are made specifically to remove grease.

Scouring cleaners are abrasive cleaners used to remove stubborn stains. These may scratch or damage finishes and must be used with caution and a light touch.

Dishwashing agents are known as dishwashing soap, dish detergent or dish soap. These are foaming agents and are formulated with low skin irritation in mind. They are used to clean glasses, plates, and utensils.

Floor cleaners are specially formulated to clean floors. Different types of floors may require different types of cleaners.

Drain cleaners are highly caustic chemicals which dissolve organic matter. If these touch skin or are ingested, they can cause serious harm.

A Cleaning Policy

Cleaning is one of the most important things that you can do to improve the health and well-being of your workforce and give your clients a good impression of your business.

Your staff spends as much as a third of their day, five days a week or more, working in your office. While there, they are exposed to whatever is in the environment.

Thus, if your office is not clean, your employees and visitors are exposed to:

- Dust which can cause allergies and illness.
- Germs which can result in an increase in colds, flus and other diseases.
- Past such as insects and rodents which can carry disease and cause other problems.

Unclean eating areas such as kitchens and cafeterias can cause an increase in foodborne diseases, mold and mildew problems, and infestations of insects and rodents.

The first thing that visiting clients see when they visit your business is your office space. If your lobby is cluttered and filthy, then the impression that your visitors receive will not be good. If your restrooms are grimy and scandalous, then you might find your clients never come back.

To prevent these kinds of issues from occurring, all companies needs a cleaning policy.

What is a Cleaning Policy?

Your organization needs policies and procedures to ensure that your staff is following best practices in cleaning. You can come up with a policies and procedures guide for cleaning on your own or engage the services of a professional cleaning company.

The Process

Believe it or not, there is a process for creating a cleaning policy that will work for your business. There's no need to overcomplicate this process, and it can usually be done in an afternoon or two.

BENEFIT/RISK ANALYSIS

What are the risks to your business for unclean environment? What are the benefits? What is being done now? Are there legal requirements for cleaning? Understanding the answers to these questions can help you come up with an effective cleaning policy that fulfills exactly what is needed for your environment.

ANALYZE THE SOLUTION

Now that you understand the risks and benefits for cleaning your face, and you know what's being done now, you can come up with an effective solution to ensure that the needs of your organization are met. Thoroughly examine any regulations and standards and come up with procedures and policies that meet the needs.

WRITE IT ALL UP

Take the time to write up your cleaning requirements in the form of policies and procedures. At this point, you're not so much concerned with who does the cleaning as to what needs to be done. The "who" is determined in the next step. Don't over complicate writing up your cleaning procedures; an outline of a page or two is probably enough at this point.

DETERMINE WHO DOES THE CLEANING

Once you understand the requirements and have a good grasp of the solutions, you can determine what can be performed by a professional cleaning company and what should be done by in-house staff.

IMPLEMENT THE POLICIES AND PROCEDURES

Finally, implement the procedures and policies as you've described them.

CONTINUE USING YOUR PROCEDURES

Don't just write up your policies and procedures and then put them on the shelf. Policies and procedures don't work if they are not put into use. Resist the temptation to relax them or stop doing them altogether.

Remember that a cleaning business is a healthy and prosperous business.

What Should be in a Cleaning Policy?

By following these steps, you can quickly come up with a cleaning policy and procedures document. First, you want to answer some questions.

Why is cleaning important to your business?

List out the reasons why cleaning is important to your business. This will help when you're justifying the costs of doing the job professionally to management.

Are there legal requirements for cleaning?

It's essential to look at any kind of legal requirements for cleaning. For example, restaurants must pass inspections regularly. If your business has any legal requirements, make sure you include them in your policy to help with understanding why cleaning needs to be done.

Do you have any team members who suffer from allergies that may require special procedures?

This is important, because team members who suffer from allergies can become very ill and their productivity can be greatly reduced. One great way to help with allergies is to

97

ensure that air vents are cleaned regularly, filters are replaced, and nonallergic cleaning supplies are used.

WHAT NEEDS TO BE CLEANED AND WHY?

Understand each of the areas in your business that needs to be cleaned and why it needs to be done. Restrooms and kitchens are obvious because cleaning prevents illnesses and diseases. Closets and equipment rooms must also be cleaned, although it can probably be done on a relaxed schedule. Rooms that are not cleaned often become clutter magnets, which can make it difficult to find equipment and other things that are stacked from floor to ceiling in haphazard piles. Additionally, pests such as insects and rodents look for dark and unvisited places to hide.

WHAT HIGH-PRIORITY AREAS ARE THERE?

Kitchens and restrooms are two areas that should be cleaned often for health reasons. Look for other areas in your office space that need to be cleaned more thoroughly or more often.

Lobbies, for example, are often the first place in your business that your customers see, so it's important that they be spotless and tidy. It's a good idea to clean lobbies and entranceways daily if possible.

HOW OFTEN DOES CLEANING NEED TO BE DONE?
Remember different areas can require different schedules. Restrooms and kitchens may require daily cleaning, and at the other end of the spectrum closets and equipment rooms may only need to be cleaned out quarterly.

WHAT AREAS ARE LOW PRIORITY FOR CLEANING?
Closets and out-of-the-way spaces may require less intense cleaning, perhaps once a month or even once a quarter.

DO YOU HAVE ANY PREFERENCES FOR CHEMICALS USED?
You might have employees that are allergic to certain chemicals, or perhaps your company prefers to use green products.

WHEN SHOULD CLEANING BE SCHEDULED?
Many companies schedule cleaning crews to come in several times a week after hours or

on weekends. Some high traffic areas, such as restrooms near the lobby, might require cleaning multiple times in a day. What times of day will those be cleaned?

ARE THERE OUT-OF-THE-WAY, SELDOM THOUGHT OF AREAS THAT SHOULD BE CLEANED BUT ARE OFTEN FORGOTTEN?
Think about ductwork, especially those venting directly onto staff members. Ducts build up dust which can exacerbate allergies, but they are often forgotten when writing up cleaning policies.

ARE THERE FILTERS, MATS AND OTHER DIRT COLLECTING SUPPLIES THAT NEED TO BE CHANGED REGULARLY?
This includes filters on air conditioners and heaters, mats in entrance ways, and so on.

ARE THERE HAZARDOUS AREAS THAT SHOULD BE TREATED WITH CARE?
Are hazardous chemicals such as flammable liquids, acids and so forth on the premises? Do these require special procedures for cleaning? Should they be inspected during cleaning?

WHAT SHOULD CLEANERS DO IF THEY NOTICE PROBLEMS?

For example, if the cleaning crew notices that hazardous and flammable chemicals have spilled on the floor or leaking, should they report that to someone, and if so who?

BENEFITS OF A CLEANING POLICY

There are many benefits to taking the time to analyze and write up a cleaning policy.

Perhaps the most important reason is to gain the understanding and acceptance by other stakeholders. Sometimes senior leaders don't understand the importance of cleaning.

To many, it's *just* a janitorial service and some even go so far as to want to make cleaning part of the responsibilities of their team members with the mistaken belief this will save money.

Of course, individual team members should be responsible for keeping their areas clean and cleaning up any messes they leave behind. If the spill happens, it shouldn't be left for the cleaning crew – it should be cleaned up immediately. Otherwise, a slip and fall accident can occur or furniture or carpets could be ruined.

But team members have regular duties to be performed, deadlines to meet, and jobs to get done.

By doing the work up front, writing up a comprehensive cleaning procedures and policies guide, you can be ready to answer any objections or questions that you may receive.

As you work through the process of getting approvals to hire a cleaning company, you'll receive many questions and objections.

WHY DO WE NEED TO SPEND THIS MONEY ON A PROFESSIONAL CLEANING SERVICE?
You can answer that is legally required or there are safety reasons for doing it or whatever you found out in your research.

WE DON'T HAVE THE BUDGET FOR THIS
You can explain how cleaning increases productivity, reduces risk from illnesses and germs, and improves the company image for clients.

WHAT WOULD THIS CLEANING SERVICE DO ANYWAY?

You'll be able to show them exactly what duties are done by the cleaning crew and which are best done in-house.

WHY CAN'T OUR STAFF CLEAN INSTEAD?

A stakeholder may ask you this question, and you'll have the answer for them.

- Cleaning involves the use of chemicals that require training.
- Special equipment that's expensive to purchase may also be required.
- Cleaning is usually done outside of regular office hours, which can be a burden to already overloaded staff.

By doing the work up front to understand the cleaning requirements and process, you'll have the answers ready for any objections or questions.

Cleaning Companies

You might think that hiring a professional cleaning service is an optional luxury. After all, how bad is it if the carpet isn't vacuumed on a regular basis and the dishes in the kitchen are washed daily? What's wrong with the few scuff marks on the wall, a dirty floor, or dusty shelves?

In any event, why can't you just ask one of your employees to do the cleaning for you? Or better yet, hire just an individual to do the job for you? After all, it's just cleaning. It can't be that hard, can it?

We've already discussed the importance of cleaning and some of the hazards of not keeping your offices and workspaces neat and tidy. I'm sure you already understand that dirty dishes piled up in your offices kitchen sink attract insects and animal pests, dust causes allergies, and a general unkempt appearance lowers morale and negatively affects the opinions that your customers have about your business.

On the other hand, clean workspaces improve morale, give customers a good first impression of your business, prevent allergies and other illnesses, and reduce stress overall.

Getting help with office cleaning is a necessity, not a luxury. Your business will suffer – meaning lost customers, reduced employee productivity, and increased incidence of illnesses – if the environment in which people work or your clients congregate is dirty or unclean.

Having said that, doesn't it make sense that cleaning is something that should be done well and by professionals? Do you really want to leave a task that important to the health of your business and employees to amateurs?

The problem with hiring individuals, even though they might appear to be more cost-effective, is they will become less responsive to your needs as their cleaning business grows. Individuals who clean must pay their bills, as would be expected, and because of that they will take on as many clients as they can. They can become overwhelmed which may reduce the quality of their services. Additionally, if for some reason they don't show up for work, there is no backup plan, so you're left without cleaning services.

Professional cleaning companies understand the importance of cleaning and they are the best option to provide these services. Their personnel have been specially trained in various cleaning techniques, understand how to use chemicals in an environmentally safe manner, and perform the job quickly and efficiently.

These companies understand their business depends on their professionalism, so they are highly motivated to get it done right. They know that leaving behind dirty carpets, dusty shelves, messy floors, and so on is not the way to gain your referral or long-term business.

Is the Cheapest Cleaning Company the Best?

If you've been in business very long, you should understand that the cheapest solution is usually not the best solution. The lowest bidder on any project or contract does not usually produce the best product or deliver the best service. After all, their prices are lower for a reason.

You might find their schedules are inflexible because they need to take on more business to make up for their lower bids on jobs. This can make it difficult to schedule around work events, customer meetings, employees working late, and so on.

Turnover may be high because they may need to pay lower rates to their employees. Minimum wage doesn't usually attract top-performing workers, and that's true with cleaning companies as well.

The training and education that they provide to their employees may be reduced or lacking entirely, especially if turnover is high. Cleaning does not imply unskilled labor. People need to be trained to use often harsh chemicals in a safe manner, they must understand how to use the equipment, and they must know the proper techniques for each different type of cleaning to be done. Scrubbing wooden floors may require different chemicals and different tools than scrubbing tile or concrete, for example.

Since finding personnel to work for low wages can be a problem, low bid cleaning companies may (but not always) hire illegal immigrants. This can introduce legal problems for your own company and is something you want to be on the lookout for.

Finally, low bidding companies may not adequately background check their employees, especially if turnover is high. This introduces the possibility of criminals having access to your facilities after hours without supervision.

This doesn't mean to say that the cheapest solution is always the worst solution. There are times when a lower bid is correct. Just ensure that you do your homework and check the references for any company that you hire.

ARE BACKGROUND CHECKS IMPORTANT?
Background checks should be a standard procedure for any business as part of their standard hiring procedure. All vendors,

especially those that have unfettered access to facilities or equipment, should be thoroughly investigated before hiring. Additionally, any contracts that you sign with any cleaning company should include a clause that background checks will be performed on their cleaning staff.

Why is this important?

The cleaning crew often works without supervision during evening and weekend hours. Because of this, it's not difficult to steal or damage your equipment or your facilities themselves.

Recently, I had a conversation with an office manager at a major retailer about this exact problem. "We noticed that equipment was disappearing. One day someone reported they were missing a laptop. Another lost their iPhone. A desktop computer disappeared, and a few iPads were missing in action. At first, we just shrugged it off as people just misplacing their equipment, but once the CEOs laptop mysteriously disappeared, we decided to investigate. We hung a few hidden cameras in the office to see what was happening when we weren't around, and soon found that one of the cleaning crew was a thief."

How Do You Find Trustworthy Cleaning Services?

A common way to find reliable and trustworthy cleaning companies is by referral, which means a recommendation from a trusted friend, family member, coworker or businessperson. Ask various people around you if they've used cleaning services and, if so, would they recommend them and be willing to share contact information.

One method to finding trustworthy cleaning companies is to visit local networking groups such as BNI (Business Networking International) and ask them for referrals. In these kind of groups, you can make a visit or two without charge. Your local Chamber of Commerce is another excellent place for referrals.

Of course, tools such as Google and other local search engines can be used to find cleaning services in your area.

If the cleaning service has an online presence, such as on Google or Yelp, read the reviews, if any. Look for patterns and reviews. There are often unsatisfied or angry customers who leave very negative reviews, and this should be taken into account. Ask yourself these questions as you're looking at the reviews:

- **Are most of the reviews negative**? Many companies receive one or two negative reviews for various reasons, and that doesn't mean that they provide bad service or products. However, if most of the reviews are negative, then perhaps you should look elsewhere for cleaning services.
- **How old are the reviews?** Consider recent reviews, because conditions change, a bad employee might be gone, management may have changed or the company may have cleaned up its act.
- **What is being reviewed?** Read some of the reviews to determine if any negatives are about services that do not apply to your circumstances.

It's important to understand that people tend to write reviews when they are angry or upset with the business. That's why on many websites you'll find a preponderance of negativity. Many customers forget to leave good reviews because they're satisfied, and it just slips their mind.

For this reason, a few bad reviews shouldn't be taken to mean that a company provides poor service. On the other hand, a preponderance of bad reviews indicates you should avoid doing business with them.

WHAT QUESTIONS SHOULD YOU ASK BEFORE HIRING A CLEANING SERVICE?

Usually, cleaning companies have unsupervised access to your business during evening or weekend hours so as not to interfere with employees and your operations. In most cases, an employee of your company isn't present while cleaning is being performed.

Because of this, trust is vital. As mentioned in the previous section, you need to ensure that background checks are done on the cleaning service employees themselves. Additionally, before you sign the contract, you need to ensure that the cleaning service itself passes minimum standards at least.

The first thing to do is to ask some questions to understand more about the cleaning service.

Are background checks performed on all employees? As described previously, ensure that background checks are performed.

Is drug testing done on employees? You should ensure that regular drug testing is performed on any employee or contractor of the cleaning company that will be working at your location. Drugs are a problem that you don't need in your business.

What training programs are in place? Professional cleaning is not a job that you can just expect anyone to do without any training or support. Ask your cleaning company what kind of training programs they have in place for their personnel, and how often people are trained and brought up to date on the newest technologies and techniques. Training should be mandatory to ensure the best service and that cleanings are well done.

Will the same employees be used each visit? This is more important than it seems at first glance. There are certain procedures that are specific to your business that need to be employed each time a cleaning is performed. You might have specific requirements based on furniture, materials, locked rooms, and so on. Constantly rotating personnel means that employees that are not familiar with your business and procedures will be doing the work. This could mean unsatisfactory cleanings are performed or procedures may not be followed as desired.

Of course, things come up and sometimes alternate employees need to be used. Vacations, illnesses and so forth do require that other cleaning people occasionally be used.

But the best practice is to keep the same cleaning crew working your facility week after week. This ensures that they understand what needs to be done specifically for your business and buildings.

What are your criteria for rates? Some cleaning services charge hourly for the initial visit because they're not familiar with your facility. Of course, the hourly charge is multiplied by the number of employees sent.

After the first cleaning, the cleaning service should have a good idea of what's required to clean your offices and other facilities. At this point, they should be able to provide you rates for each visit and for optional services. These rates will change based on how much work needs to be done to provide the service, how often you need the service, and what services are performed.

Understand how rates are calculated before you sign any contracts or before they start work. That way there will be no surprises.

Is the cleaning service insured and bonded? This is not optional. Any business, and especially professional cleaning services, needs to carry liability insurance, and be insured to cover breakage, damage and theft.

This will eliminate any problems or confusion when (not if) something is broken, damaged, or even stolen.

Who is responsible for the equipment and supplies? Professional cleaning services should be responsible for supplying their own equipment and obtaining supplies. That should be part of the cost of the service.

Does the cleaning company carry workers compensation? This is important because you don't want to be liable for any injuries that occur while cleaning.

Is there a guarantee? Ensure your cleaning service provides a guarantee of your satisfaction. What will they do if you don't feel a cleaning job was done properly? Will they redo the cleaning at no charge? Under what circumstances can you terminate your contract? Make sure you understand precisely what happens when things go wrong. Even with the best companies and personnel, accidents happen.

What services do they provide? Ensure that everything you need done is covered under their service. If you need the patios cleaned, for example, then make sure that's included in your contract. Otherwise, you might find yourself stuck with some unexpected charges because of services that you expected that are not included.

What hours will they work? Make sure the cleaning service will perform their duties on a day and time that's convenient for you and your business. Generally, cleaning services work after hours or on weekends so they don't interfere with employees and clients.

What about on unplanned visits? If your business needs to be cleaned outside of the normal schedule day and time, how is that handled? Is there an extra charge, and if so, how much? Do they need advance notice? Will they use the same crews? Unexpected things happen, so make sure you understand your options.

How long have they been in business? Is this a new company, or has it been around a while? If it is a new company, what are their credentials? A brand-new company might still be setting up shop or working out how to run a business. This could result in inferior service in the short term, although not necessarily so. On the positive side, they may give you a discount just to get your business.

How long is the agreement? Is the contract month-to-month or does it last for a period such as a year? Generally longer contracts command a lower price because you're giving the cleaning company a guarantee that they'll get your business for that period. Month-to-month has the advantage in that you can change companies at will if needed.

How can you terminate the contract if you're unhappy? Make sure your agreement with the cleaning company specifies the conditions under which you can terminate the contract, how much notice needs to be given, and the reasons you must give for termination. Can you terminate if you're unhappy? Or does it require proof of poor cleaning? These are all important things to know before you sign.

Do they provide references? If they can't give you some references, find a different cleaning company. Of course, even if they give you references, they're going to give you the names and phone numbers of customers satisfied with their service. Even so, call those references and get into a conversation with the responsible person at those businesses. Find out, if you can, what they really think about the services they receive.

Get it all in writing. Any agreements that you make with your cleaning company need to be in writing in a contract. Ensure this written agreement specifies everything that you expect your cleaning company to do, and everything that you discuss with them. As they say, oral agreements are worth the paper they're written on. To prevent disagreements or misunderstandings, make sure everything is in writing and go over it thoroughly with your cleaning company to ensure that both of you understand.

History of Cleaning

When I was a child, my parents taught me the value of cleaning by insisting that my room be tidy before I was allowed any luxuries such as dessert or an extra treat. They also took the time to explain to me why they had a focus on cleanliness.

Because of that, I never had any issues with keeping my room clean and well kept. Sure, I was an active young man, doing all the things that a child and later a teenager does – sports, friends, hiking in big bear, and working odd jobs.

But because I understood the reasons behind clean living, I always took the time, well, almost always, to clean things up regularly.

People all over the world associate the concept of being clean and remaining clean with health, well-being and competence.

Believe it or not, people didn't always clean using the tools and technology that we have today. Oh sure, of course they didn't have vacuum cleaners and other equipment that we take for granted, but even the methods they used were different because of different technology, social customs, and beliefs.

EGYPT

When most of us think of Egypt, we think of pyramids, mummies, Ramses, Cleopatra, and similar things. Yet the ancient Egyptians valued cleanliness in their environment and their grooming. (Sailors, 2018)

Just look at the way they treated their dead. The organs were carefully removed, and the body wrapped in cloth. Once that was done, their dead were buried in tombs where they could remain unmolested for, presumably, the rest of eternity.

The upper-class Egyptians attached much importance to cleanliness. They even appointed a royal supervisor to oversee laundry, and this person was a prominent member of the court. Of course, the act of washing clothes was considered degrading, so that was done by lower-class individuals. (Hays, 2012)

The Nile supplied Egyptian cities with water, which led to the invention of bathing. You can see this in paintings which show bathers being surrounded by attendants pouring water on them.

BABYLON

The Babylonians understood the dangers of contaminated water and knew that it could cause diseases and illnesses. Because they were close to the Tigris and Euphrates rivers, they can use the water daily for regular activities in their household, including cleaning. Slaves carried handheld jars from the river to be used by their upper-class masters.

The streets of Babylon built up deposits of excrement, dirt, filth and so forth. Occasionally, this was covered up with a layer of clay, causing the streets to slowly rise to a level higher than the houses they were servicing. This is the reason many homes have stairs leading down to their doorways. (Plumbing Supply, 1989)

GREEKS

The Greeks kept slaves who oversaw cleaning. They used water from springs, and frequently scrubbed down possessions such as statues to ensure they looked as good as new.

The Greeks even created the term "miasma", which means to pollute. In later times, this morphed into a more general meaning for foul air. They also created the word "hygiene" which means creating conditions that prevent disease and improve health.

ROMANS

The Romans brought in freshwater to their cities by using aqueducts, then built sewers to get rid of used and unclean water. They also built public and private baths to allow people to keep their bodies clean.

MODERN TIMES

Closer to modern times, Leeuwenhoek, Koch and Pasteur discovered microbes, and showed how they could be transmitted in human and animal populations.

People have "always known quote that rot and filth leads to disease and illness, and science has come after the fact to prove that this is true.

Since then, technologies such as vacuum cleaners, washing machines, dishwashers, antiseptics, and so on furthers the goal of removing bacteria, cleaning up filth, and creating a clean environment.

REVEREND MARTIN LUTHER KING JR.
The influence of the civil rights movement on sanitation and cleanliness is interesting, especially in Memphis, Tennessee. (Dreier, 2017)

In the 1960s, Union such as the United Auto Workers and International Ladies Garment Workers donated money to civil rights groups. These unions helped organize the 1963 March on Washington – the same one where Martin Luther King Junior delivered the famous "I have a dream" speech.

Because of his reputation and standing in the community, the Memphis civil rights and union leaders asked Rev. King to come to Memphis to garner national attention to their ongoing garbage strike.

On January 31, 1968 it all began because 22 sewer workers were mistreated. It had been raining, and the white employees were sent home and received pay. On the other hand, black workers didn't get paid for the day.

The next day, a malfunctioning garbage truck crushed Echol Cole and Robert Walker to death. The situation escalated over the next month because of the mistreatment of black sanitation workers. The mayor and the city Council refused to help, and on February 12, 1,300 black sanitation workers went on strike.

Thousands of tons of garbage piled up on the streets. Nonunion workers and supervisors were used, but even so there was not enough manpower to make up the difference.

As the situation escalated for the next month, the city refused to budge. Finally, on March 18, Rev. King spoke at a rally and asked everyone to remain nonviolent. On March 28, King led a march, and police tried to break it up and arrested 280 people, injured 60, and shot a 16-year-old boy.

Martin Luther King delivered a speech on April 3 at the Mason Temple in the city to over 10,000 black workers, residents, ministers, white union members, white liberals and students. This was his last speech as he was assassinated the next day by James Earl Ray.

After this, President Johnson intervened and ordered federal troops to Memphis. On April 16, union leaders finally reached an agreement with the city. After that, the African-American community became more involved in local politics

Future of Cleaning

New technology is changing the world ever more quickly.

- Smart manufacturing is allowing for the automation of entire factory floors that are almost completely unmanned except for a few supervisory personnel.
- Self-driving cars are already a reality and will soon be commonplace on roadways.
- The first self-driving semi-truck was recently tested, and it won't be long before entire fleets of automated, unmanned trucks carry cargo across the United States.
- Amazon uses robots to store and retrieve products from massive warehouses.
- Automated ships that are entirely without crews will soon make an appearance to carry cargo across the oceans.
- And I'm sure we were all fascinated to watch the recent SpaceX launches and

the boosters that landed themselves on unmanned drone ships at sea.

How does the advance of technology affect the mundane and unglamorous world of cleaning? Will there be changes that may cleaning more effective, more environmentally safe, and cheaper?

ARTIFICIAL INTELLIGENCE

Artificial intelligence is already being used in robotic vacuum cleaners. The iRobot Roomba uses AI to scan a room, identify obstacles, and remember routes to do the best cleaning. These robots understand about obstacles and changing conditions, and they know how much cleaning they can do with the amount of power left in the battery.

In the future, the applications for artificial intelligence and cleaning are wide open. Floor cleaning robots will be able to recognize when certain areas require deeper cleaning, such as with a stain or some gum stuck in the carpet.

Air conditioning ducts may be installed with small robotic cleaners that constantly keep the ductwork clean of dust and debris.

Restrooms and kitchens will include built in automated cleaning devices to keep sinks, toilets, dishwashers, and refrigerators always sparkling clean without the need for human intervention.

All these applications require artificial intelligence combined with robotics, because the robots require an understanding of the layout of a room, and air conditioning duct, a sink, refrigerator or other location. They need to understand differences in debris, stains or dirt that they find and know what type of cleaning needs to be done. They must also adapt to changing conditions, such as furniture being moved around, pets, children, or people at a party.

Artificial intelligence will completely change the way cleaning works over the next decade, eliminating or reducing many of the labor-intensive tasks.

FLOOR CLEANING ROBOTS

Cleaning a floor is over 95% labor. Because of this, robot floor cleaners – especially vacuums – have become popular in the past few years.

Commercial floor cleaning units are also appearing, and allow for unsupervised cleaning of hotels, hospitals, airports, and so forth. These robots use sensors – laser scanners and ultrasonic detectors – to detect obstacles. These robots can operate without supervision and can clean hundreds of thousands of square feet each day.

In the future, buildings will be designed to aid cleaning robots in their tasks. Special optical cables and transmission devices could be installed throughout the building to help the robots identify where they are, where they need to clean, and what's left to do.

Duct Cleaning Robots

Air ducts are one of the dirtiest places in a home or business. These tubes collect dust and debris which raises cooling and heating costs and can directly cause allergies and breathing problems.

Unfortunately, cleaning ducts is expensive because it's almost entirely a manual effort and special training is required.

Robots are being developed that can enter through existing openings and perform the cleaning tasks. Currently, these robots are remotely controlled by human beings, but in the future, they will autonomously clean ducts without intervention by people.

WINDOW CLEANING ROBOTS

Several robots have been designed to clean outside the windows on skyscrapers. This makes sense, because that kind of window cleaning is extremely dangerous to human beings.

These robots use belts of suction cups to secure themselves to the glass as they clean. They do a better job than human window cleaners, and they can perform their tasks regardless of the weather, the wind, or other conditions.

MEDICAL CLEANING ROBOTS

Hospitals harbor particularly nasty cleaning conditions. Just think about all the germs growing on every conceivable surface from all the illnesses and sick people in the building.

Medical cleaning robots use special UV lights to disinfect rooms. These robots are wheeled around by housekeepers then left alone in the room to do their cleaning.

City Wide of Memphis

City Wide is the premier building maintenance company in the United States.

Memphis resident and entrepreneur Scott Romero owns and operates City Wide of Memphis to give local business and building owners optimum service for commercial maintenance.

City Wide of Memphis manages all vendors, fields all service calls, and negotiates contract rates to remove the burden of building maintenance from business owners. This allows those owners to focus on the most important thing for them – managing and operating their business.

Services provided include:

BLINDS CLEANING

Blinds accumulate dust more quickly than virtually any other area of a business. This is because they are consistently stationary, allowing dust to accumulate over time. City Wide provide services that get your blinds and window coverings back to their original appearance. Additionally, they can provide repairs and replacement services.

CARPET AND UPHOLSTERY

Dirt, dust and germs accumulate inside the fibers of your carpeting. This makes your rooms dirty and reduces the effective life of your carpeting. Additionally, dust and dirt within carpets are a leading cause of allergies.

City Wide can provide a regular program of cleaning and ongoing maintenance to protect your carpets and keep them looking their best for longer.

COMMERCIAL CLEANING

With over 55 years of experience cleaning commercial properties, City Wide has the expertise to clean any building. We understand what you need out of your cleaning services and will put together the best service agreement possible for the unique needs of your business.

We work with virtually all industries, including:

- Auto dealerships

- Banks
- Churches
- Commercial offices
- Daycare centers
- Dialysis clinics
- Healthcare facilities
- Schools
- And just about any other type of business you can imagine.

We take care of the management of maintenance and commercial cleaning vendors for you, so you don't have to deal with any of the details.

CONSTRUCTION CLEAN-UP

Construction projects create large amounts of dust and huge amounts of debris and messes. City Wide offers construction cleanup services for just about any situation. We'll haul away debris and complete the finishing touches to get your latest construction project done so you can open for business on time.

DETAIL CLEANING

Perhaps you have a high-profile client coming to visit your company, or the CEO is stopping by, and you need a thorough, very detailed cleaning. City Wide will be happy to help you create and execute a plan to get your business in tip top shape, managing the right crews, and make sure your building is as clean as it can be.

FLOOD RESTORATION

Flooding can be a major disaster, and can cause serious damage to floors, walls, furniture, and anything else in your business. City Wide is available to help you restore your property and manage water damage cleanup.

Our services in this area include:

- Water Damage Repair
- Pipe Repair
- Office Clean-Up
- Water Remediation and Carpet Drying
- Emergency Water Extraction
- Carpet Repair and Replacement
- Mold Remediation
- Deodorization
- Stain Removal

Floor Care

Floors are important, because they are the first thing that anyone sees when they enter your business. A dirty floor, or even one that doesn't shine like it used to, says a lot to prospective customers.

Ongoing maintenance is a vital part of keeping your floors looking good and lasting as long as possible. We work with all floor types including hardwood, ceramic tile, VCT, marble or any other surface.

We provide all the services:

- Burnishing
- High-Performance Vacuuming
- Installation and Removal
- Refinishing
- Repair
- Scrub and Wax
- Strip and Wax

We also work with specialty floor types such as:

- Cement and Epoxy Floors
- Gymnasium Floors

- Hardwood Floors
- Marble and Terrazzo
- VCT and Ceramic Tile
- Warehouse Floors

HANDYMAN

Every business has a list of small repairs, maintenance tasks, and decorating projects that never seem to get done. After all, you have a business to run, and who has time to patch a small hole or fix a broken doorknob?

City Wide can help you by performing all these handyman tasks. We do everything from patching and painting to minor repairs to providing supplemental labor. Just give us your to do list, and we will take care of it.

JANITORIAL SERVICES

Our primary mission at City Wide is to ensure that you receive excellent janitorial service, stellar response, and professional experiences. We make sure that any time spent on janitorial in your building is on task, efficient, and complete. You will never see full trash cans or dirty floors after we finish working.

Janitorial Supplies

City Wide can take care of your janitorial supplies, by making sure that you never run out of toilet paper or soap or other essentials. Your City Wide Facility services Manager will ensure your building is always stocked with these vital supplies so you never run out.

Kitchen Cleaning

Many businesses include a kitchen or cafeteria on site. These require special attention because cross-contamination with food preparation can be unsanitary and lead to infections and disease. Taking the proper precautions and doing the appropriate cleaning is vital. City Wide works with experienced and knowledgeable vendors to make sure your kitchen is serviced properly and safely.

Matting Services

Your entryway is one of our highest priorities. We recommend that entryway mats be used as a common supplement to janitorial services. These prevent slip and falls by anyone entering your building. Additionally, shoes carry contaminants such as bacteria and dirt, and entryway mats help prevent this dirt from getting further into your building.

City Wide can get you mats in a wide variety of materials and styles – we can even provide them with your company logo. You can either purchase them or sign up for a scheduled matting service that replaces them on a regular basis.

MOLD REMEDIATION

Any time a facility experiences water damage or you notice an unusually musty odor, you may be at risk of mold contamination. Molds affect indoor air quality and they can produce toxins that cause serious health risks.

Mold grows in any place where moist air condenses including bathrooms, kitchens, basements and so on. Fixing mold problems isn't easy. Fortunately, City Wide works with crews who use safe and effective equipment and methods in accordance with or exceeding industry standards to help you clean up whatever mold problem you may be experiencing.

PEST CONTROL

In the summer, mosquitoes, silverfish, flies and cockroaches can be a problem for businesses. In colder raining months, cracks, crevices and other openings at your facility must be sealed to reduce the risk of pest infestations.

To keep pests at a minimum, prevent the following from occurring:

- Open garbage cans/trash areas
- Unattended debris/landscaping outside your building
- Unsealed doorways or windows
- Food left out in break rooms and offices

Even with the best measures, insects and other pest sometimes slip through the cracks. City Wide has access to pest control experts who can come out to your building to evaluate for potential problems and provide the appropriate solutions.

SECURITY AND ACCESS CONTROL

City Wide provides for all your building access needs and concerns. We install new systems, keys, locks and do ongoing maintenance. We can work with you to help you create a security plan that fits in your budget and addresses your needs.

TENANT IMPROVEMENT

For property managers, the needs of tenants take priority. This can mean expansion, division or alteration of the facility. We work with expert commercial and office renovation specialists who can take you through the process and take care of the details, so you can focus on your business. We will manage the process from beginning to end, using contractors who are trained and experienced in their field.

WORKPLACE WELLNESS

By choosing City Wide as your janitorial service, you can rest easy knowing that your cleaning, sanitation, and disinfectant needs are taken care of. We will work with you to ensure your facility is proactively treated before, during and after the cold and flu season. We also manage a wide variety of workplace wellness services to help you prevent illnesses in the workplace.

CONTACTING CITY WIDE OF MEMPHIS

Call City Wide of Memphis today so we can talk to you and work out a plan to provide the optimum janitorial services for your business.

Conclusions

Throughout this book I've stressed that cleanliness is important to all businesses.

Some of the reasons include:

- A clean business is a prosperous business.
- Clean offices are staffed by happier employees.
- Lobbies that are maintained and cleaned attract and impress customers.
- Cleanliness directly affects your bottom line.
- Buildings that are clean and kept up attend to last longer and have fewer maintenance problems.
- Employee illnesses and time off for sicknesses are reduced in a clean building, especially if kitchens and bathrooms are regularly scrub down.

A professional cleaning company, who hires skilled janitorial professionals, understands the value of clean and well-kept office spaces.

They also understand the dangers of chemicals, pests, allergens, and so forth. That's one of the advantages of using professionals instead of doing the cleaning yourself – professionals have been trained and have the experience to know the importance of doing cleaning correctly and safely.

Sometimes it's difficult to get all the stakeholders including management to understand the value of cleaning and furthermore, the necessity for hiring professionals to do the job.

One of the primary purposes of this book is to give you a good grounding in the facts about cleaning so you can effectively create and build a case for using a professional cleaning company, or at least ensuring that cleaning is done regularly, even if it's done by your own internal staff.

City Wide of Memphis provides professional janitorial services and commercial cleaning services to all kinds of businesses. If you need professional services of this nature, give us a call will be happy to help you.

References

Abrams, A. (2017, August 23). *Your Cell Phone Is 10 Times Dirtier Than a Toilet Seat. Here's What to Do About It.* Retrieved from Time: http://time.com/4908654/cell-phone-bacteria/

Adams, A. (2017, August 23). *Your Cell Phone Is 10 Times Dirtier Than a Toilet Seat. Here's What to Do About It.* Retrieved from Time: http://time.com/4908654/cell-phone-bacteria/

B-Air. (2017, September 29). *A Comprehensive Guide to Cleaning Commercial Floors.* Retrieved from B-Air: https://b-air.com/2017/09/how-to-clean-commercial-floors/

CCOHS. (n.d.). *Sanitation and Infection Control for Cleaning Staff.* Retrieved from Canadian Centre for Occupational Health & Safety: https://www.ccohs.ca/oshanswers/hsprograms/cleaning_staff.html

Charpentier, W. (n.d.). *Safety Hazard Analysis of Custodial Jobs.* Retrieved from Chron: https://work.chron.com/safety-hazard-analysis-custodial-jobs-11461.html

Dreier, P. (2017, December 6). *Why He Was In Memphis.* Retrieved from Huffpost: https://www.huffingtonpost.com/peter-dreier/why-he-was-in-memphis_b_5088614.html

Five Hazards of Professional Cleaning. (2016, December 27). Retrieved from CleanLink: https://www.cleanlink.com/news/article/Five-Hazards-of-Professional-Cleaning--20159

Hays, J. (2012, January). *Clothes, Fashion, Hygiene and Sex in Ancient Egypt.* Retrieved from Facts and Details: http://factsanddetails.com/world/cat56/sub365/item1939.html

MediaBeast. (2017, March 11). *What is the Best Way to Clean Commercial Flooring?* Retrieved from ServiceMaster Restore: https://www.servicemasterofcharleston.com/what-is-the-best-way-to-clean-commercial-flooring/

Organic Consumers Association. (n.d.). *How Toxic Are Your Household Cleaning Supplies?* Retrieved from Organic Consumers Association: https://www.organicconsumers.org/news/how-toxic-are-your-household-cleaning-supplies

Plumbing Supply. (1989, July). *The History of Plumbing - Babylonia.* Retrieved from Plumbing Supply: https://www.plumbingsupply.com/pmbabylon.html

Sailors, M. (2018, July 12). *The Incredible History of Cleaning.* Retrieved from Maidsailors.Com: https://maidsailors.com/blog/incredible-history-cleaning/

Singh, K. (2014, June 29). *4 Household Items To Clean Your Phone With.* Retrieved from Mashable: https://mashable.com/2014/06/29/household-items-to-clean-phone/#9N3C45KUhPq1

The Health Site. (2015, June 30). *How dirty is your phone?* Retrieved from The Health Site:

https://www.thehealthsite.com/diseases-conditions/how-dirty-is-your-phone/

Zhu, B. (. (2013). Environmental Disorder Leads to Self-Regulatory Failure. 19: December.